Learning to read. Reading to learn!

LEVEL ONE Sounding It Out Preschool–Kindergarten
For kids who know their alphabet and are starting to sound out words.

learning sight words • beginning reading • sounding out words

LEVEL TWO Reading with Help Preschool–Grade 1
For kids who know sight words and are learning to sound out new words.

expanding vocabulary • building confidence • sounding out bigger words

LEVEL THREE Independent Reading Grades 1–3
For kids who are beginning to read on their own.

introducing paragraphs • challenging vocabulary • reading for comprehension

LEVEL FOUR Chapters Grades 2–4
For confident readers who enjoy a mixture of images and story.

reading for learning • more complex content • feeding curiosity

Ripley Readers Designed to help kids build their reading skills and confidence at any level, this program offers a variety of fun, entertaining, and unbelievable topics to interest even the most reluctant readers. With stories and information that will spark their curiosity, each book will motivate them to start and keep reading.

Vice President, Licensing & Publishing Amanda Joiner
Editorial Manager Carrie Bolin

Editor Jordie R. Orlando
Designer Luis Fuentes
Text Jessica Firpi
Reprographics Bob Prohaska

Chief Executive Officer Andy Edwards
Chief Commercial Officer Brett Clarke
Vice President, Global Licensing &
  Consumer Products Cassie Dombrowski
Vice President, Creative Dov Ribnik
Director, Brand & Athlete Marketing Ricky Melnik
Account Manager, Global Licensing &
  Consumer Products Andrew Hogan
Athlete Manager Chris Haffey

Published by Ripley Publishing 2020

10 9 8 7 6 5 4 3 2 1

Copyright © 2020 Nitro Circus

ISBN: 978-1-60991-400-4

For more information regarding permission, contact:
VP Licensing & Publishing
Ripley Entertainment Inc.
7576 Kingspointe Parkway, Suite 188
Orlando, Florida 32819
Email: publishing@ripleys.com
www.ripleys.com/books

Manufactured in China in March 2020.

First Printing

Library of Congress Control Number: 2020931349

PUBLISHER'S NOTE
While every effort has been made to verify the accuracy of the entries in this book, the Publisher cannot be held responsible for any errors contained in the work. They would be glad to receive any information from readers.

WARNING
Some of the stunts and activities are undertaken by experts and should not be attempted by anyone without adequate training and supervision.

PHOTO CREDITS

Cover (tl, tr, cl, cr, bl) Photography by Mark Watson; (c) Photography by @nicolasjacquemin; (br) Photography by Chris Tedesco; (l) © Bashkirev Yuriy/Shutterstock.com; (r) © Bashkirev Yuriy/Shutterstock.com; (bkg) © EFKS/Shutterstock.com **3** Photography by @nicolasjacquemin **4-5** Photography by Phil Lagettie **6** Ziyaad Douglas/Gallo Images/Getty Images **7** (t) Photography by Jarno Schurgers; (b) Photography by Mark Watson **10-11** Photography by Sam Neill **12-13** Photography by @nicolasjacquemin **14-15** Photography by Mark Watson **16-17** Photography by Mark Watson **18** Photography by Chris Tedesco **20** Photography by Mark Watson **21** Photography by Mark Watson **22-23** Photography by Sport the library/Jeff Crow **24-25** Photography by Mark Watson **26-27** Photography by Mark Watson **28-29** Photography by Mark Watson **30-31** Photography by Jarno Schurgers

Key: t = top, b = bottom, c = center, l = left, r = right, bkg = background

All other photos are courtesy of Nitro Circus. Every attempt has been made to acknowledge correctly and contact copyright holders, and we apologize in advance for any unintentional errors or omissions, which will be corrected in future editions.

NITROCIRCUS
GO BIG!

RIPLEY
PUBLISHING
a Jim Pattison Company

Nitro Circus is a group of men and women who perform stunts.

They ride bikes and scooters all over the world.

Lots of people come to see them.

Riders go fast to fly up
and come down.

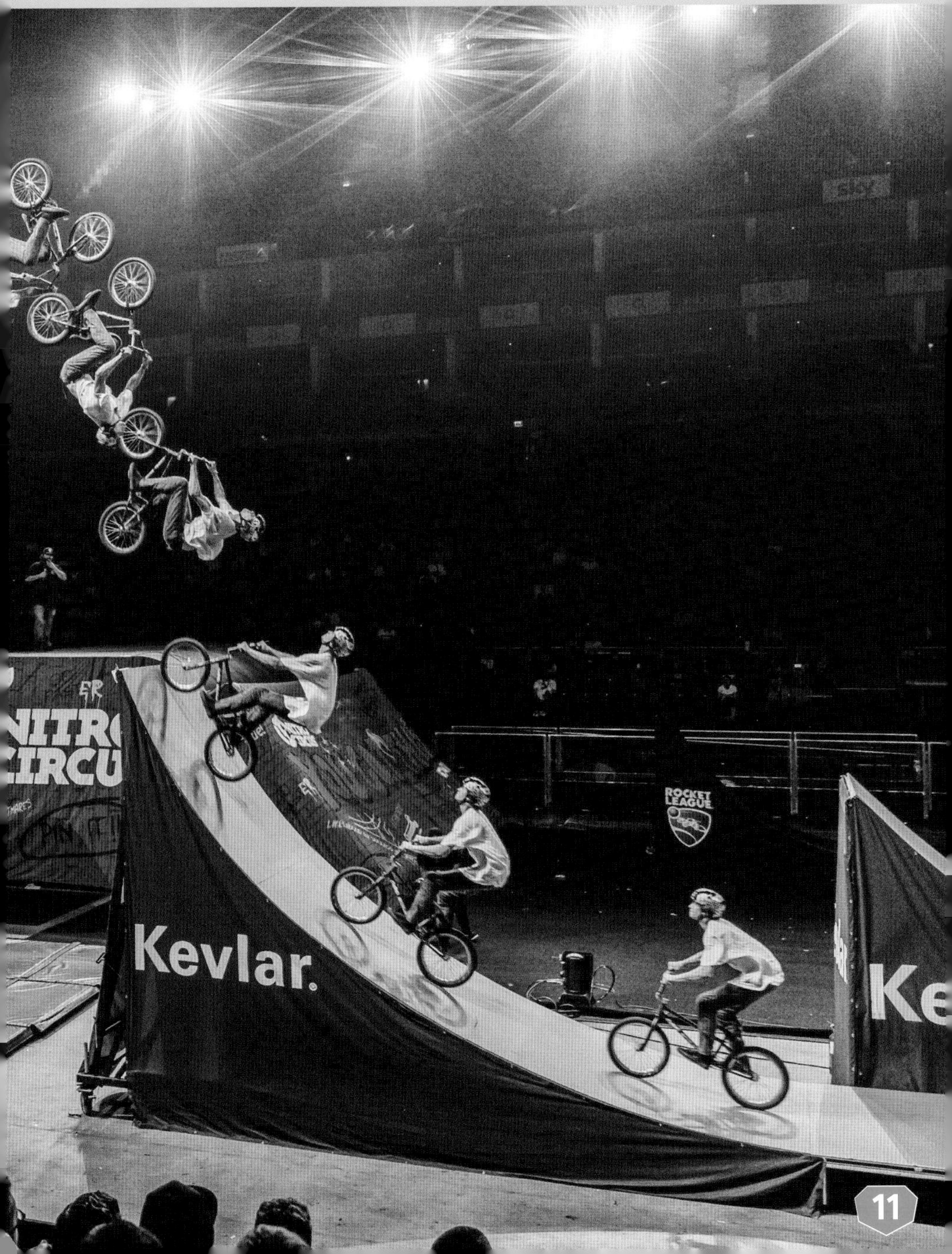
Kevlar.
ROCKET LEAGUE

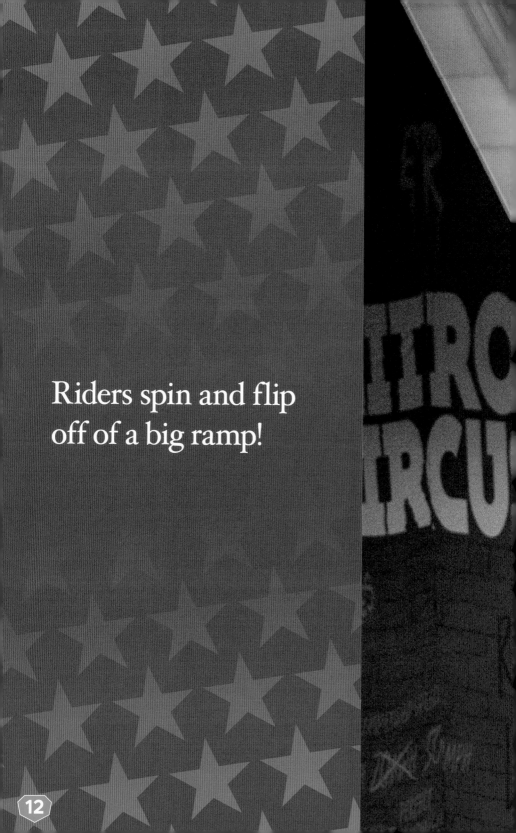

Riders spin and flip
off of a big ramp!

They do it over and over again.

Some land on soft bags of air.

Others do cool tricks
on all kinds of things.

Look at the chair and the boat!

It is very hard.

Not many riders can do it.

Many riders jump close to fire!

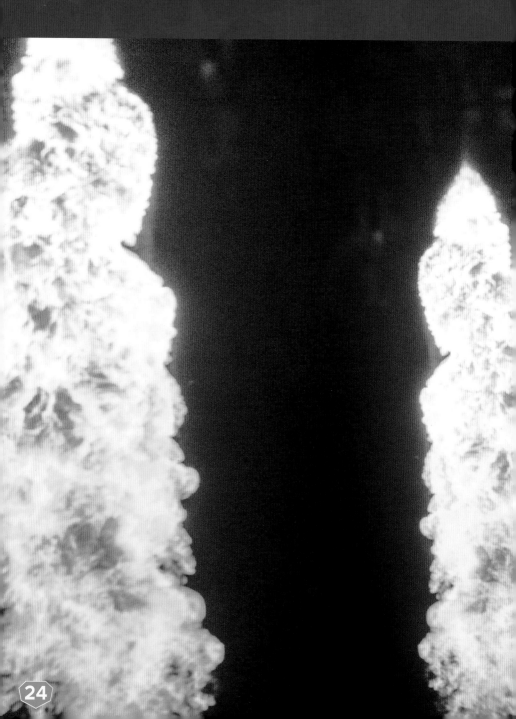

Every rider jumps at once.

So cool!

See the riders go!

See the crowd cheer!

So much fun!

Ripley Readers

Ready for More?

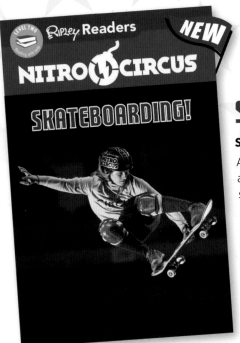

SKATEBOARDING!

Skateboarding is so much fun!
And so is learning how the athletes at Nitro Circus ride, jump, and spin their skateboards. Strap on your helmet and prepare to read about some amazing tricks, the professional gear, and the "you got this" attitude of skateboarding at Nitro Circus! Ripley Level 2 Readers are perfect for kids who know their sight words and are learning to sound out new words.

Learning to read. Reading to learn!

 Reading With Help
Preschool–Grade 1
- expanding vocabulary
- building confidence
- sounding out bigger words

 Independent Reading
Grades 1–3
- introducing paragraphs
- challenging vocabulary
- reading for comprehension

For more information about
Ripley's Believe It or Not!, go to www.ripleys.com